The Soul Rescue Manual:
Releasing Earthbound Spirits
by Patrick Rodriguez

Table of Contents

Welcome to the Soul Rescue Series.

This Soul Rescue Series Manual is a current work-in-progress. Your comments and feedback are both welcomed and invited.

I also invite you to share your Soul Rescue experiences about what happens after reading the Manual!

Relax, enjoy and have fun, you're about to learn and participate in the remarkable field of Soul Rescue.

Please know that your comments and book reviews are very much appreciated. They help other people in making the decision to buy this book. If you've found this book valuable please consider leaving a book review.

Amazon.com

And please visit my website for information, products and videos on Soul Rescue and Spirit Release.

www.SoulRescueSite.com

With love and appreciation,

Patrick Rodriguez

Chapter 1.   Introduction Biography

I began with a background of NLP, hypnotherapy and in-depth spiritual studies. After my first experience in communicating with earthbound spirits, I felt that I had finally become in touch with my true Life Path.

I will often work with mediums to guide and assist them in developing their skills in channeling spirits in a respectful and compassionate manner.

I have developed Scripts that virtually anyone can use to help spirits to transition. Using principles from each of my past disciplines, I teach the students of the Soul Rescue to apply his or her intent when using the various scripts.

The primary method of helping earthbound spirits is through conversations. In advanced studies of Soul Rescue that spirits can be assisted to transition by finding the spirit's own individual issue then helping the spirit to heal or resolve that issue in order to move to the Light.

This manual is the product of my experiences of working with several psychic-mediums, which I refer to only as mediums throughout this text. Throughout the text I use the term "we" when relating to experiences I've had when working with these talented mediums. They all have my gratitude for their help and participation in the countless Soul Rescue sessions that we've experienced together.

Chapter 2.   Goals & Outcomes

The goal of this book is to learn effective methods of assisting earthbound spirits to transition to the Light. You will start with a simple approach of learning to "Call Out" spirits and progress to learning advanced methods of communicating with spirits through a medium, or channel.

You will learn how earthbound spirits become trapped within homes and properties and how even newly constructed homes or buildings can house spirits. You will also learn how earthbound spirits can attach to living people and the methods of how to release these spirits in a safe manner.

You will become adept at learning the effects of the presence of earthbound spirits on living people. The goal of this book is to help you to recognize these effects in order to find opportunities to assist spirits to transition. The goal is never to evict or "get rid of" the spirits.

The Soul Rescue Manual will start with an easy-to-learn method of calling out to wandering earthbound spirits that are willing and ready to transition. We will then progress into theories and methods of release for trapped spirits ("hauntings") and spirits attached to living people. During each part of the teachings you will have opportunities to participate in exercises aimed at releasing earthbound spirits.

Throughout the various exercises we will be focusing on earthbound spirits that are willing to transition. The second part of the series begins to prepare student teams to work with stubborn spirits and spirits that, at first, may not be willing to transition.

Chapter 3. First time experiences as a medium

In the first part of the book we will be inviting wandering earthbound spirits that would like help in transitioning to come and be present. This immediately sets our intent for the remainder of the manual for assisting these spirits to transition into the Light. This is also an invitation to the reader to begin exploring your own intuitive and mediumship skills.

When doing these exercises in a class setting, different participants will feel various levels of changes in the room or see different things appear. As each participant shares an experience, this often opens new levels of awareness for others. Someone may share that they felt cold coming from a certain area in the room. Another person may share that they saw a bright light. What invariably happens is that other people will become conscious of what they saw as well, although they were not aware of what they were initially seeing or feeling.

Many people have had experiences of seeing, hearing or sensing disincarnate beings at some point in their lives, prior to attending these classes, but without having been consciously aware of what they were experiencing.

This book will give you an active conscious experience of interacting with disincarnate beings.

Hearing Footsteps, Noises and Feeling Presences

Most people do not usually think of mediumship as the same as hearing "ghosts". It's not an uncommon experience for many people to feel the presence of disincarnate beings or to see and hear things from no logical source.

Spirits will often make their presence known to living people. It is important to remember that many earthbound spirits simply do not know, or acknowledge, that they are dead. They may have a strong compulsive desire to simply communicate with the living, partially so that they can feel alive again. In many cases the spirit simply wants to be acknowledged and to feel connected to others at a human level again.

Natural Mediums and Learned Mediums

A Natural Medium is a term that is often used to describe a person that can see or hear spirits without training. These individuals are often highly gifted psychics and have usually developed other intuitive senses as well.

Other people have found that by participating in the active exercises of Soul Rescue, that they have developed latent mediumship abilities. It is not uncommon for participants to easily channel spirits within the first attempt.

Some people will never consciously have the ability to see or hear spirits, although intuition and perception may be developed as a result of participating in Soul Rescue sessions. These individuals often make excellent facilitators. As the manual progresses the reader will find how he/she interacts best in this work.

Please note that it is absolutely NOT necessary to have any mediumship abilities to greatly help many earthbound spirits.

Opening the Doors to Communication

One aspect to experiencing the conscious phenomenon of interacting with spirits is opening the awareness to any subtle changes in the environment. It is easy to dismiss a cool breeze that may happen during a Calling Out exercise. It might be easy to rationalize a speck of light out of the corner of the eye when asking for Angels to appear. Most people will be quick to suggest looking for a logical explanation or physical cause to the experience. In Soul Rescue we first look for spirit validation.

As an example, when a facilitator calls for Angels, s/he may see, what is believed to be, lights fluttering in the corner of the room. As the facilitator turns to stare in the direction of the corner there appears to be string hanging from the ceiling. Does this mean that there were no lights actually fluttering?

By allowing various experiences to simply be observed, you may begin to observe and experience communication happening at various subtle levels. Keeping an open mind is key in Soul Rescue and will allow you to fully experience the beauty and mystery of the spirit world.

Chapter 4. The Life After Death Cycle and Lost Souls

To discuss Earthbound Spirits, or Lost Souls, we must first understand the normal process of what happens when a person dies.

From countless books, movies and television programs, many people have been made aware of the Near-Death-Experience (NDE). Dr. Raymond Moody in his classic work, Life After Life, chronicles the experiences from over 150 people who have clinically died or almost died.

According to the experiences of these NDE survivors, the spirit will separate from the body and is typically met by a tunnel or a white light. Beings of Light, or Angelic Beings, will meet the spirit to guide him or her in the transition. Very often the spirit will recognize these beings as departed loved ones from his or her lifetime. This is what we refer to as the Normal Life-After-Death Cycle.

In other instances the spirit will separate from the body, but finds some urgent or pressing matter that is more important than the transition towards the Light. For many of these spirits it is the desire for "another chance", or revenge, or a multitude of personal reasons unique to that individual that will keep him/her earthbound. This is not a decision, per se, but rather an unconscious thought process that happens instantaneously.

In one instant a man may be driving his car feeling tired and sleepy. In the next instant he may be wandering through space and time, unaware of where he is or how he arrived there.

In one spirit session we were introduced to a man that was soon to be a first-time father. Harry had been out celebrating with co-workers on the night that he died. He was exhausted from the long hours he had recently been putting in at the office. His last memory was seeing headlights coming at him, and then only remembering that he needed to get home to his expecting wife. It was the tremendous guilt of leaving his wife that had kept Harry earthbound. By releasing the guilt, Harry was then able to make his transition.

Earthbound Spirits typically will not consciously choose to stay behind. Rather, it is the emotional attachment that keeps the spirit stuck between worlds. Many spirits will wander searching for explanations of how they became stuck between these two worlds.

Many spirits are not aware that they no longer have a physical body. These spirits often become sad, angry, resentful, discouraged or a number of other "negative" associated feelings. One reason that has been given for these feelings is the frustration that no one can see or hear them. For many earthbound spirits, eternity becomes nothing more than a mournful experience of existence.

Some living people find that they have the ability to see or sense spirits but "turn off" or "tune out" this ability. Often spirits will be attracted to these people with the unique ability to see or communicate with spirits and will attempt to establish contact with them. Some spirits, in an effort to try to communicate with people, will make noises, move personal belongings or try to make his or her presence known in many different ways. The person who has consciously, or unconsciously, chosen to shut-off this skill may often wonder why spirits seem to be attracted to homes that they live in or places where they go. In some cases, the spirits are only looking for recognition or for help.

As a student of Soul Rescue, you will learn techniques and methods for helping earthbound spirits to transition, or crossover.

Chapter 5.   Calling Out to Wandering Earthbound Spirits (EB's)

In this section we will now prepare you for your first experience in assisting earthbound spirits to transition to the Light. I refer to the role of coordinating the spirit release as the Facilitator. Many people have been pleasantly surprised at how simple, and yet effective, this process can be using the technique found in this manual.

In this first lesson you will simply read from the script, out loud, with the intent of assisting the spirits to transition. As the lessons continue, more knowledge and information will be assimilated. By understanding and applying the intent of the Script you will soon find that you are able to assist greater numbers of spirits and with greater finesse.

Preparation: The first part of this exercise is a very key aspect of the process. You must be in a "centered" state that allows you to speak to spirits in a compassionate and direct tonality. Note that as you become increasingly confident in using the Script, you should strive to develop an "authoritative tonality". A visual image of this tonality is exemplified in a kind police officer directing traffic. He/she instills confidence in the person driving but does not appear overbearing in his/her approach.

The first part of this exercise is a very key aspect of the process. You must be in a "centered" state that allows you to speak to spirits in a compassionate and authoritative tonality.

1.   Take a few moments to breathe and become centered

2.   Let go of any fears of the process

3.   Let go of any disturbing thoughts or concerns not associated with the task at hand

Releasing Earthbound Spirits Script

"I ask for Healing Angels and Guardian Angels to please come now and I ask for protection for myself and all that are here so that no new attachments are incurred as a result of the work that we are about to do.

"I ask for Healing Angels and Angels of Transition to please come now and be present for all the spirits that will be called here.

"I now invite any spirits that would like help in transitioning and are ready to transition to please come now.

"I ask that all the Earthbound Spirits here be told, in a way that they can understand, that their physical bodies are no longer in existence but that they continue to exist.

"I ask that they be told, in a way that they can understand, that they are worthy and deserving of going to the Light and that there is no judgment waiting for them except that which they put on themselves.

"I ask that they be helped now to release any judgment on themselves and allow the angels to take away the hurt, guilt and judgments.

"I ask that the angels please heal any their aches and sorrows and I invite all you spirits to let go of your hurts, depression or any other pains to the angels.

I now invite all the spirits here to forgive those that they feel they need to forgive from any hurt in the past. Allow the angels to help you with whoever needs to be forgiven so that you can easily move on.

"I now call upon angels of transition and transitioned loved ones to lovingly come for all the spirits here and escort them to the Light.

"Thank you.

"Angels, I ask now that you please remove any residues left by any of the spirits from this space and from myself and all those present. Thank you. Amen"

Chapter 6.   Earthbound Spirits and Soul Rescue

Spirit Guides vs. Earthbound Spirits

At times, Earthbound Spirits can be confused with Spirit Guides. Some people will choose to not Release spirits from their home or energy field because they feel that if a spirit is present, then that spirit must have a higher purpose for being there.

It has been my experience that many spirits do have intent to aid or help living people in some manner; however, the non-transitioned earthbound spirit is limited to the knowledge and insight gained from his or her most recent incarnation. By contrast, the transitioned Spirit Guide has received specialized training in how to help the person in his/her charge and has learned distinct rules and guidelines that must be followed for the highest good of the person in his/her care.

A Spirit Guide may offer advice in the form of intuition to a person. If the person chooses to disregard the intuition, the guide will simply respect the choice and wait for another opportunity to be of service. A Spirit Guide will have a long-term view with the wisdom gained from the experience in the Light with other guides, masters and Angelic Beings. By contrast, an earthbound spirit will usually only understand the choice within the context of his or her own life; tainted by his/her own desires, aversions and emotional attachments.

Transition to the Light (Crossing Over)

The goal of assisting the spirit to Transition to the Light, or crossover, is the primary outcome of the Soul Rescue process. In the advanced levels of Soul Rescue we will discuss methods and techniques of assisting the spirits with healing of physical residues, forgiveness, neutralizing multi-life karma and other healing methods.

It is important to always keep in mind that, although we would like the spirit to heal, the primary outcome is Always to help the spirit to transition. All other healings are secondary. This distinction will become important in subsequent advanced trainings.

Angel Help

Angels are used in Soul Rescue for the healing of physical residues of the spirit's last incarnation, which is usually related to how he or she died, and/or the emotional healing of the spirit, which is usually some form of sadness, anxiety, etc. Angels are also called on to escort the spirit to the Light for the transition. We assume that the spirit can readily see the Angels when making a request.

Angels make the process easier for both the Facilitator and the spirits that will be transitioning. More will be discussed about the interactions between the spirit and the Angels in subsequent chapters.

Healing and Forgiveness

Although healing may not be required in order for the spirit to transition, this step will often make the process easier for the spirit. Healing may come in the form of physical residues, emotional pain or even as new mental or logical understanding.

In one case, a woman appeared looking like a zombie from a typical Hollywood low-budget movie. This is rarely how spirits will show themselves. In this woman's case she was continuing to perceive herself the way she had died, which was drowned and still lying at the bottom of a river.

In most cases they appear just as they had when they were alive, just before their death. We immediately called for Angels to clear out the dirt from her mouth, throat and body. We also asked that she be cleaned and dressed in the outfit of her choice. The physical-residue healing of the spirit allowed the session to progress very easily from that point forward.

Often a spirit will feel that he or she is not able to move on because they are immersed in feelings of, "Why me?" or "What did I do to deserve this?" In situations where these feelings become a block for the spirit we ask the Angels to show the spirit what was the Originating Cause for his or her experience.

During a class demonstration, we once encountered a man that would not leave because he was angry with the driver of a vehicle who had killed him during a hit-and-run accident while the (then living) man was on his bicycle. We asked the Angels to show the spirit the Originating Cause of the experience. The spirit was very surprised (almost shocked) to find that the driver and himself had been involved in numerous lifetimes together where each had taken the other's life. In this last lifetime it was simply the other man's turn to kill him. In a previous life he had been driving a chariot and the other man had been run down. Karma was simply replaying itself once again. We asked the man if he would be willing to forgive the driver of the vehicle for the hit-and-run, and all the previous lifetimes that he had been killed by the man, so that he could end this cycle of murder and revenge. The spirit readily agreed and we asked the Angels to assist the man in forgiving the driver and to end the karma between the two. This was a logical-mental healing for the spirit that allowed him to accept the transition. The emotional healing of forgiveness was an added bonus that will hopefully add a positive impact on the two souls in future incarnations.

Reincarnation & Physical Healing

Rarely are the physical residues an issue for the spirit to transition; however, when a spirit experiences an unusually harsh physical or traumatic death I feel that it is appropriate to ask for Angels to heal any residues from the death of the last lifetime.

In the work of Past-Life Regression Therapy (PLRT), many therapists have found that often symptoms of physical problems have been able to be overcome or greatly decreased by reliving and relieving the pains from past-life traumas. A migraine headache or knee problem may stem from an old accident or wound. A chronic sore throat may have originated from strangling, hanging or choking in a past life.

By asking for the Physical Residue Healing of a spirit it is the intent that, should the spirit choose to reincarnate, they will not need to re-experience any symptoms related to their last death.

There may be situations when the spirit may not want to address a physical issue for healing, because to do so he or she would need to address a sensitive emotional issue. In these cases, the physical issue is directly related to an emotional issue. The facilitator-medium team will then need to determine if the issue is preventing the spirit from transitioning.

During one related session, a spirit had not been willing to deal with the issue of venereal disease. To heal this issue would mean that he would have to address the emotional insecurities associated with the issue. At the same time it was this issue that was preventing the spirit from transitioning. Angels were called to help the spirit see what could be the possible outcomes from his decision of not addressing this issue. In an instant, the spirit was shown several possible scenarios that could manifest in future lives. This was not meant to serve as punishment but rather as "karma" or, a way to release the emotional charge associated with the life issue. Given the conscious choice between the option of facing insecurities and the possible lifetimes as shown by the Angels, the spirit chose to address his insecurities and heal. This then allowed the spirit to transition, free from the physical issue.

Chapter 7.   Angels & Healing

Working Models

Within the Soul Rescue work we will introduce several "Working Models", including the mythology of Angels. It is not the intent of this work to claim or present an All-Knowing-Truth, but rather to offer methods and techniques to assist earthbound spirits with the transition process. All views presented in this work are offered as Working Models and the reader is invited to accept all material as such.

Angel Mythology

The mythology of Angels that we present is that God, the Creator, created many beings, creatures and entities. The Angels were the beings created independent of God, but still of the most similar vibration energy to the Creator's own energy of love and acceptance.

In this mythology, the Angels are divided into different groups with varying job functions. Various other authors have categorized these different job functions as defining the Angels into groups called phyla. Within the work of Soul Rescue the emphasis is not to attempt to understand the various functions, or phyla, of the Angels, but only to apply the working model that Angels do have different functions and to call on the specific group of Angels that is needed during the session.

Within this Working Model of Angels, there are various groups of Angels specifically created to serve God by being of service to mankind. It then becomes the birthright of every person to be able to call upon Angels for assistance, either for themselves or for another group of people or person.

Angel Help

There are many other methods of Soul Rescue, taught by other authors and practitioners, that will not involve the use or calling upon Angels; however, I have found that the method of using Angels simplifies and expedites the process in a holistic manner.

Angels will come instantly upon request and can perform several types of immediate healings for the spirit. Angels can also work in the lives of the living, although without the dense physical form, the spirit will be instantly aware of the changes with Angel healings.

In advanced Soul Rescue, the Facilitator will ask the Angels to bring new awareness or understanding to the spirit in certain areas that are holding the spirit back from transitioning.

Calling on Angels

In the work of Soul Rescue we primarily call upon three groups of Angels; Guardian Angels, Healing Angels and Angels of Transition.

Guardian Angels are asked to protect the people performing the Soul Rescue and the location so that any spirits that do not choose to transition will not linger in the location or with the persons performing the release.

During some sessions, other earthbound spirits may simply be curious about the work being done or may have past-life issues with the spirit having the session. The Guardian Angels will also prevent these spirits from interrupting or interfering with the spirit session.

Healing Angels are called to assist the spirit in removing physical residues such as aches and pains or even residues from bodily injuries, such as from car accidents or gunshot wounds. These Angels will be asked to assist the spirit to remove emotions such as sadness, depression, anxiety or whatever emotion is preventing the transition.

The Healing Angels can also be asked to assist in the process when a spirit needs to undergo an exceptionally hard process such as forgiving someone or remembering a past life to heal an originating cause or event.

Angels of Transition are called in advance to be present when starting a Soul Rescue. The intent of having these Angels present is to alleviate the fear of some spirits that the facilitator is trying to evict them in any way. At the end of the process, these Angels are asked to guide and escort the spirit into the Light.

Angel Limitations: Angels and Freewill

In my work in Soul Rescue I have seen very few limitations of Angels; however, the primary boundary that the Angels consistently keep is to always honor the freewill of mankind. We must keep in mind that even though a request is made for the healing of a spirit, if the spirit does not want to be healed, the Angels will respect the freewill of the spirit.

Angel Limitations: Specificity

A surprising limitation that I've experienced in asking for Angel assistance has been the need to ask with specificity. Although it is sufficient to ask the Angels to, "heal the spirit," it becomes exponentially more effective to ask the Angels to, "heal the spirit from the physical residues from the gunshot wound and any emotional or mental residues associated to the event."

In this mythology of Angels, all is perfect and there is no need for healing. They will respond to requests, but they will not interfere with the experience of mankind unless they are asked to do so.

Spirits seeing Angels

The Facilitator must trust in the process that the spirit(s) will immediately see and recognize the Angels when the Angels are called in to assist. When using the generalized Calling Out, the Facilitator acts as a coordinator, orchestrating the healing and release of spirits with the help of the Angels.

When working in teams, there will be spirits that are not yet ready for the help of the Angels. The spirit then will either not see the Angel, producing a scotoma (a temporary blind spot preventing him/herself from seeing the Angel) or will simply ignore the presence of the Angels, choosing instead to converse with the Facilitator.

When speaking to spirits within a home, or with a living person, the spirits may be asked to "make your presence known to the Angels so that they can help you." Although the Angels can see the spirits, this enables the spirit to give his/her consent to be helped by the Angels. This becomes a very useful practice when performing a generalized calling out of spirits.

Chapter 8.   Repeat - Calling Out Wandering EB's

In this section we will repeat the exercise from Chapter 5. Calling Out to Wandering EB's.

This is to once again practice assisting earthbound spirits to transition to the Light. The key to becoming effective in using this technique is developing the Intent of each step within the Releasing Earthbound Spirits Script.

In this second exercise you will draw from the knowledge and information in the preceding chapters to develop the intent within each part of the Release Script. Try to place emphasis on Calling Out and speaking to the spirits while reading from the script.

Calling Out & Intent

Two dictionary definitions for the word, intent:

1.   The state of mind with which an act is done

2.   Having the mind, attention, or will concentrated on something or some end or purpose

In developing the intent of Calling Out to earthbound spirits, we are aiming for developing a fully congruent will that affects our thoughts, words, voice tonalities and even our body posture. For some people this will be a loving and inviting way of Being, while for others this will be a direct, forceful and reassuring manner of Being. Each person will develop his/her own intent in a manner that matches his/her own congruent personality. For everyone, the key is to be able to congruently Call Out and reach as many earthbound spirits as possible to assist them in their transition.

Parts of using the Script

Preparation: The first part of this exercise is a very key aspect of the process. You must be in a "centered" state that will allow you to speak to spirits in a compassionate and direct tonality. Note that as you become increasingly confident in using the Script, you should strive to develop an "authoritative tonality". A visual image of this tonality is exemplified in a kind police officer directing traffic. He/she instills confidence in the person driving but does not appear overbearing in his/her approach.

1.   Take a few moments to breathe and become centered

2.   Let go of any fears of the process

3.   Let go of any disturbing thoughts or concerns not associated with the task at hand

Angel Protection Request: The next step is inviting angels to be present and asking for protection. This is a precautionary step to prevent the wandering spirits from staying with the person or groups involved with the session.

Calling Out to EB's: Earthbound spirits that are ready and willing to transition are then invited to come. During this step it is normal to feel dips in temperature, feelings of sadness or depression, or other bodily-sensory experiences. This is a normal occurrence when one or more spirits enter a room. It is important to continue with the process when this happens.

Informing EB's that the Physical Body is Dead: Start by asking the Angels to tell the spirits that their physical bodies are no longer in existence (dead). The request is made in this way so that the information can come in a gentle way individually to each spirit. This information is often a revelation to the spirits and when speaking directly to the spirits (in advanced sessions), you must learn to be understanding and respectful that the spirit is often either not aware of a physical death or has been in denial over the loss of his or her physical body. In either situation, the news of their death can sometimes become a momentary harsh awakening to the spirit.

Informing EB's that they are Worthy and Deserving: Ask that the spirits be told by the Angels that they are worthy and deserving of going to Heaven, or to the Light, and that there is no judgment waiting for them. Often this is what holds a spirit earthbound; the belief that he or she is unworthy or that there is some judgment or punishment waiting for them.

Request for Healing for EB's: Ask that the Angels heal the spirit in one, or more, of the manners within the Script for two reasons. First, assume that reincarnation is a possibility. With this basic assumption, I have found in working with people using Past-Life Therapy, that many people suffer from psychosomatic, or real, illnesses or discomforts that originated in past lives. By asking for the healing of the spirit before transitioning, the belief is that this will help the spirit to not experience any condition associated with the emotion or physical residue in future lives. Second, by assisting the spirit to receive healing from the Angels we make it easier for the spirit to take the next step, which is to trust the Angel escorts to guide him or her into the Light for the transition. In this first step the spirit is simply receiving healing from some residual physical condition or emotional pain. This is typically easier for the spirit to initially accept than the transition. By first receiving healing from the Angels the process of trusting and accepting assistance to transition from the Angels becomes a natural progression.

Inviting the Transition: In this step we make the presupposition that all of the earthbound spirits that are present will choose to transition. This is a subtle but important distinction. Once again, we are like the kind and compassionate police officer directing traffic. We are respectful and compassionate, while also being authoritative (in advanced lessons). We ask for transitioned loved ones and Angels of Transition to guide the spirits to the Light. When asking for loved ones to come, we specify that we are asking for transitioned loved ones. This focuses our intent to prevent earthbound or other loved ones from interfering with the process.

Removing Residues: The final step in using the Script is to ask for the removal of any residues left by the spirits from the room, space and all people present. We have found that by asking for the residues to be removed there will be a subtle but noticeable shift in the room.

Releasing Earthbound Spirits Script

"I ask for Healing Angels and Guardian Angels to please come now and I ask for protection for myself and all that are here so that no new attachments are incurred as a result of the work that we are about to do.

"I ask for Healing Angels and Angels of Transition to please come now and be present for all the spirits that will be called here.

"I now invite any spirits that would like help in transitioning and are ready to transition to please come now.

"I ask that all the Spirits here be told, in a way that they can understand, that their physical bodies are no longer in existence but that they do continue to exist.

"I ask that they be told, in a way that they can understand, that they are worthy and deserving of going to the Light and that there is no judgment waiting for them except that which they put on themselves.

"I ask that they be helped now to release any judgment on themselves and allow the angels to take away the hurt, guilt and judgments.

"I further ask the angels to please heal each one of any past residues from their death so that they need not experience any symptoms in any future life. I ask that the angels please heal any their aches and sorrows and I invite all you spirits to let go of your pains to the angels.

I also now invite all the spirits here to forgive those that they feel they need to forgive from any hurt in the past.

"I now call upon angels of transition and transitioned loved ones to lovingly come for all the spirits here and escort them to the Light.

"Thank you.

"Angels, I ask now that you please remove any residues left by any of the spirits from this space and from myself and all those present. Thank you. Amen"

Chapter 9. Trapped EB's In Houses & Properties

What makes an EB "Haunt" a property?

Earthbound spirits will often find places, persons or groups of people that resonate with their own desires, aversions or personalities. A spirit may be attracted to the busy preoccupation of an office environment because that is how they spent their life. Another spirit may have simply enjoyed shopping as a preoccupation and now finds themselves in shopping malls.

There will be countless individual reasons why a spirit will become trapped in a physical location, but usually the core reason is that the spirit resonates with the energy of the person, people, building, and/or location.

It is important to remember that most spirits are not malicious in any manner, but they can at times become curious. A spirit is simply a person without a physical body that has become "lost" or "trapped" between the world of the physically living and the world of the after-life.

Does an EB have to have died in the house?

Among paranormal investigators, a common procedure is to research public records for previous owners of a home or property to find the previous owner(s) that may match the qualities of the spirit(s) now haunting the property. However, it has been my experience that spirits do not need to have died in the home or to even have had a physical connection to the property in order to chose to dwell there.

One experience I had was a spirit that was residing in a home had been a fisherman. James had lived in poverty most of his life. His little fishing shack was adequate for his needs but the drafty shack lacked the warmth and luxury of his new home. Unfortunately for James, a medium and I had been asked to clear the home of spirits. James, knowing that he had been squatting in the home, readily agreed to transition after the Angels told him that the room he was occupying was now needed by others. James' only regret was that he couldn't take the plush, velvety curtains with him.

How do you know if an EB is trapped in a house?

There will be several potential signs of spirit activity if spirit visitors are suspected of being in a home or property. The most common activity is the feeling of being watched or feeling the presence of another person in the room, usually late at night or when alone and with no other activity competing for attention. Many people have also reported hearing footsteps or knocking sounds on walls as a sign of spirit presence.

In relatively rare cases, spirits have been known to move or hide physical objects, manifest in the form of mist or shadows, float objects, tamper with electronic equipment or turn appliances on or off, among other things. If you should encounter any of these extreme cases I recommend contacting a practitioner trained in Attached Spirit Release for the release or clearing of the property.

How is the release different?

When calling out to wandering spirits to assist them in the transition, most spirits responding to the invitation are already ready and willing to crossover.

In working with spirits trapped within properties, the spirit may feel safe within the confines of his/her known world, which may only be a specific bedroom or corner office. The key in assisting these spirits is to make the process emotionally safe for them and, with the help of the Angels, constantly reassure the spirit(s) that the new home will be even better and safer than their present location.

During one session, the spirit of Mary had been channeled by the medium. Mary was unaware that she had died but enjoyed painting in her garden. Mary was caught in that one forever-moment painting in her garden, waiting for someone to acknowledge her or share her existence.

As we spoke with Mary we discovered the tremendous loneliness that she experienced in the garden, which was now holding her captive. However, when we told Mary that she no longer had a physical body and that she could transition, she surprisingly declined to go at first.

The garden and the painting had become her safe haven and she was reluctant to leave it so easily. As we emphasized the loneliness that Mary was feeling in her existence, we then offered that the Angels could show her a new home where she could be at peace and also experience the company of loved ones as well.

Mary made a beautiful transition with the help of the Angels.

Will the Calling Out method work on homes & properties?

The Calling Out method (using the Release Script) is an excellent technique for assisting willing spirits to transition. Often spirits that are trapped within homes and properties will transition if given the opportunity of going somewhere better.

Some spirits will need more specific assistance before they are willing to transition. For these spirits, sometimes just talking to them and helping them to understand that they no longer have a physical body is enough to begin the transition process. Details of this will be covered in the Working In Teams section.

Chapter 10. Releasing EB's From A Home or Property

In this section we will practice calling out to earthbound spirits trapped within a specific location and assisting the spirits to transition to the Light.

This exercise works best if you have someone to work with, such as a friend or family member. The reader will be the Facilitator and the other person will be the client. The Facilitator will be releasing spirits from the home or property of the Client.

The facilitator will draw from the knowledge and information in the preceding chapters to develop the intent within each part of the Release Script. In this exercise the facilitator will place his/her intent on speaking to the spirits within the home or property of the Client.

The Exercise

This exercise will be done in teams of "Client" and "Facilitator".

The Client will focus on his/her home (or a home that s/he is intimately familiar with).

The Facilitator will release the EB's from the Client's home (or a home that s/he is intimately familiar with).

Client; focus on the home and give a brief description to the facilitator.

Facilitator; follows the intent of the client's focus to the home.

Optionally the facilitator can pretend that s/he can see or sense the client's home. Ask the client for more details if necessary. The intent of the facilitator is to call Angels to that home and to speak to the spirits residing in, trapped, or attached in the home.

The first part of this exercise is a very key aspect of the process. In this exercise, both the Client and the Facilitator must take time before starting to become centered. The Client must visualize, or sense, his/her home or location. The facilitator must be in a "centered" state that allows him or her to speak to spirits in a compassionate and authoritative tonality.

1.   Take a few moments to breathe and become centered

2.	Let go of any fears of the process

3.	Let go of any disturbing thoughts or concerns not associated with the task at hand

The next step is inviting angels to be present and asking for protection. This is a precautionary step to prevent the wandering spirits from staying with the person or groups involved with the session.

Proceed with reading from the script.

Releasing EB's From A Home or Property Script

Sample prayer/request - Calling Out to Release Earthbound Spirits from a home or property

I.	Prepare Yourself Mentally and Emotionally

II.	The Script

"I ask for Healing Angels and Guardian Angels to please come now and I ask for protection for myself and all that are here and there so that no new attachments are incurred as a result of the work that we are about to do.

"I ask for Healing Angels and Angels of Transition to please come now to the home of (client's name) and be present for all the spirits there.

"I now invite all the spirits there in the home of (client's name) to make their presence known to the angels.

"I ask that all the Earthbound Spirits there be told, in a way that they can understand, that their physical bodies are no longer in existence but that they continue to exist.

"I ask that they be told, in a way that they can understand, that they are worthy and deserving of going to the Light and that there is no judgment waiting for them except that which they put on themselves.

"I ask that they be helped now to release any judgment on themselves and allow the angels to take away the hurt, guilt and judgments.

"I further ask the angels to please heal each one of any past residues from their death so that they need not experience any symptoms in any future life. I ask that the angels please heal any their aches and sorrows and I invite all you spirits to let go of your hurts, depression or any other pains to the angels.

"I also now invite all the spirits there to forgive those that they feel they need to forgive from any hurt in the past. Allow the angels to help you with whoever needs to be forgiven so that you can easily move on.

"I now call upon angels of transition and transitioned loved ones to lovingly come for all the spirits there and escort them to the Light.

"Thank you.

"Angels, I ask now that you please remove any residues left by any of the spirits from the home of (client's name) this space and from myself and all those present. Thank you. Amen"

Chapter 11. Introduction to Attached Spirit Release (ASR)

The Purpose of Attached Spirit Release (ASR)

The practice of ASR is based on mental and emotional health and recovery. The premise is that, for many people, their own core emotions and issues can become amplified by the presence of disincarnate spirits or other entities. By assisting these spirits and entities to transition the client is then freed of the amplified emotional charge and is then able to deal with only his or her own issues. As a result of this practice we have also seen psychosomatic illnesses and emotional symptoms released almost overnight.

Symptoms of Spirit Attachment include, but are not limited to:

- Chronic lack of energy for unknown reasons

- Chronic psychosomatic ailments for unknown reasons

- Symptom or condition that does not respond to traditional healing methods

- Out of control emotions and outbursts

- Abrupt behavior changes

- Fast mood swings

- Hearing voices

- Addictive behaviors or tendencies

- A feeling of "Something seemed to take over" or "It was like it wasn't me doing that"

A person with an attached spirit can often take on the illness symptoms or personality traits that the deceased person had while alive.

Psychosomatic Symptoms

An Earthbound Spirit may retain the energy residues from physical maladies experienced in their life. When attaching to a living person, the living host may experience what has come to be known as psychosomatic illnesses.

These are illnesses that have been unable to be treated or diagnosed in conventional medicine. A traditional physician will often refer a patient with these symptoms to psychologist or other professional for therapy.

Often these types of illnesses have cleared up using Attached Spirit Release.

Just Trying to Help

Perhaps the best way to illustrate the How and Why an Earthbound Spirit may become attached to a person would be to share my own experience. When I began my work with Spirits, I had no idea that my first client in doing Spirit Release would be myself.

My story begins with my father. He was an alcoholic with drastic mood swings that shifted with his intoxication binges. On any given day he may have been a caring father and later that same evening turn into an abusive tyrant.

As a child of only about eight years old I didn't know how to handle these mood swings of my father. I was angry and hurt that he would abuse me but I could not voice my feelings or stand up for myself at that age.

During one such episode while I was curled in a fetal position with fear, Robert stepped into my life. Or should I say, Robert stepped into Me.

Robert was an Earthbound Spirit. In life he was big, powerful and direct. He was caring to me but could stand up to my father. When my father began to drink, it was now Robert who stood in-between us. It was Robert who took the abuse but it was also Robert who tried to protect me from getting hurt by influencing my decisions to keep people at a distance. After all, in Robert's world you can't get hurt if you don't let people in.

For much of my life this became my own way of dealing with people, including those I loved. I never allowed myself to get too close to anyone.

By the time I got a chance to meet Robert, he was ready to leave. I told Robert that I appreciated his intervention when I was a child. I let him know that I now understood his intent in coming into me at that time. I also let him know that now that I was an adult I was much better prepared to take care of myself. I explained to him that it would be best for both of us if we now parted company.

All communications with Robert were conveyed with caring and respect. He agreed to leave and Angels were invited to escort him to the Light.

ASR & Soul Rescue

By using the principles and techniques of Soul Rescue, many spirits can be assisted to transition and this also may help alleviate many challenges from the living host. In advanced Soul Rescue, the facilitator-medium teams will learn to call out and speak to spirits that are affecting a living host with a specific issue or challenge.

Chapter 12. Calling Out Attached EB's

In this section the student-facilitator will practice calling out to earthbound spirits attached to a living person and assisting the spirits to transition to the Light. This exercise will consist of teams of client and facilitator. The facilitator will be releasing spirits from the client.

The facilitator will draw from the knowledge and information in the preceding chapters to develop the intent within each part of the Release Script. In this exercise the facilitator will place his/her intent on speaking to the spirits attached the client.

The Exercise

This exercise will be done in teams of client and facilitator.

The facilitator will release any earthbound spirits willing to transition with the help of angels and transitioned loved ones.

Client: At the appropriate point of the script, the client will speak directly to the attached spirits. The client will give thanks to the spirits that had the intent of trying to help in some way. Then make the statement that s/he is now willing to take responsibility for his/her own life and give his/her permission and blessings for the attached spirits to leave with the angels.

Facilitator: In this exercise it is the job of the facilitator to make the spirits feel SAFE. This is NOT an exorcism. The exercise is not attempting to "evict" the spirits from their home within the client. The first step is to offer the spirits help and healing from the angels. Remember, very often spirits have the intent of trying to help. Honor and respect that intent.

The first part of this exercise is a very key aspect of the process. The facilitator must be in a "centered" state that allows him or her to speak to spirits in a compassionate and authoritative tonality.

1.   Take a few moments to breathe and become centered

2.   Let go of any fears of the process

3.   Let go of any disturbing thoughts or concerns not associated with the task at hand

The next step is inviting angels to be present and asking for protection. This is a precautionary step to prevent the wandering spirits from staying with the person or groups involved with the session.

Proceed with reading from the script.

Calling Out Attached EB's Script

"I ask for Healing Angels to please come now and I ask for protection for myself and all that are here so that no new attachments are incurred as a result of the work that we are about to do.

"I ask for Healing Angels and Angels of Transition to please be present for all the spirits that will be called here tonight.

"I'm now speaking to all you spirits inside of (client's name).
I know that many of you are with (client's name) to help him/her in some way or in some cases to feel safe or protected. I'm inviting you now to receive healing from the angels that are here before you."

Client Script - Permission to Release

"I'd like to acknowledge all the spirits within me. I know that many of you have come in order to try to help me in your own way. I want to thank you now for your intent of trying to help me.

"I want you to know that I am now willing to take responsibility for my own life and I now give you my permission and my blessings to leave in the loving care of the angels."

Facilitator (cont.)

"I ask that all the Earthbound Spirits here within (client's name) be told, in a way that they can understand, that their physical bodies are no longer in existence but that they continue to exist.

"I ask the angels to please heal each one of any past residues from their death so that they need not experience any symptoms in any future life. I ask that the angels please heal all of their aches and sorrows and I invite all you spirits to let go of your hurts, depression or any other pains to the angels.

"I ask that they be told, in a way that they can understand, that they are worthy and deserving of going to the Light and that there is no judgment waiting for them except that which they put on themselves.

"I ask that they be helped now to release any judgment on themselves and allow the angels to take away the hurt, guilt and judgments.

"I also now invite all the spirits within (client's name) to forgive those that they feel they need to forgive from any hurt in the past. Allow the angels to help you with whoever needs to be forgiven so that you can easily move on.

"I now call upon angels of transition and transitioned loved ones to lovingly come for all those here and escort them to the Light.

"And as the spirits leave from (client's name), I further ask the angels to please fill those spaces with God's Love and God's Light so that nothing or no one else can get in.

"Angels, I ask now that you please remove any residues left by any of these spirits from (client's name), this space and from myself and all those present.

"Angels I ask that (client's name) suffer no ill effects in either general well being or in physical health. I also ask that if any soul fragments are available or any pieces that they be cleaned and reintegrated at their own pace or entrusted to the angels for integration at a later time when (client's name) is ready them. Thank you, Amen."

Chapter 13. ASR: Targeted Release vs. Surface Release

The Resonance Principle

Spirits are attracted to living hosts that resonate with their own challenges and/or issues. An out-of-control angry person is likely to attract out-of-control angry spirits. A person with sad and depressed tendencies is likely to attract sad and depressed spirits.

Attached EB's & Amplified Emotions

In many cases, an attached spirit that has become triggered within a person may be acting out his or her own emotions, independent of the living host. As the spirit starts to act out his/her emotions, this in turn begins to affect the emotions of the living host.

As an example; as a host becomes hurt or frightened over a situation in his/her life, s/he may have the desire to drink alcohol on a regular basis in order to cope with the pain. This pattern may awaken, or trigger, the emotions and patterns of an attached spirit. This spirit in turn may begin to amplify the host's own painful emotions and even desire to consume alcohol and become uncontrollably intoxicated. When the spirit is released from the host, the living person is then left with only his/her own emotional issues and released from the amplified emotions (or in some cases, symptoms) of the spirit.

Remote Release vs. Client Involvement

A common practice among many practitioners in Spirit Release is applying Remote Release work. This is the release of spirits from a host without the host's involvement, or sometimes even without the host's conscious awareness. This practice is often very effective, but I've come to realize that by asking the host/client to become involved in the release, there is an additional healing affect in the process.

A client/host may participate in the release as a medium, a facilitator or simply as an observer to the release. When working with an ASR team, the client will have the opportunity of hearing the story of an attached spirit's issues and what prevented him/her from transitioning In almost every case, the client will resonate with the experience of the spirit. In many cases, the client may even feel like the experiences of the spirit closely relate to the experiences or issues in the client's own life. This process of observing the session can be highly therapeutic for people and several clients have reported greater awareness of their own issues, personal growth and the ability to take greater personal responsibility for the resonating issue in their life.

My own preference is to always work with the client's participation (often by telephone conference call); however, the main goal is for this work to be made available to as many people as possible. Not everyone is ready to be confronted with the personal responsibility implied when having a release session. Although not everyone will choose to participate, it is my belief that all can benefit from a release, including the earthbound spirits.

Releasing EB's Associated with Emotions

Initially, you will learn to Call Out to attached spirits that are willing to transition. In Part II, you will learn to work in facilitator-medium teams that will be calling out to speak to spirits that would like to transition but need help in some specific matter.

Advanced ASR teams will learn to release spirits with resonating emotions. This practice is recommended only for advanced student teams due to the potential complexity of the release.

Soul Rescue, Part II – Adv. Soul Rescue & Working in Teams

Chapter 14. Working As A Team

Working as a Team

Most people today practicing various forms of Spirit Release or Soul Rescue will assist the client into a relaxed mindset using hypnosis techniques, and then ask that person to act as a medium-channel. However, using a trained medium yields significantly more in-depth results than using an untrained individual as the channel for Spirit Release and/or Soul Rescue.

A trained medium will have the ability to allow more of the personality of the spirit to come through. This makes it easier for the facilitator to interact with the spirit and to get a feeling for the personality of the spirit. Using a trained medium also will help the spirit to transition in an easier manner because this provides for a greater exchange between the facilitator and spirit.

The Facilitator Role

The facilitator is the person in charge of the release. The facilitator is in control of the situation, the discussion, the healing and the manner in which the release unfolds.

The word facilitator could be interchanged with coordinator. As in the Practice Sessions in using the Script, the facilitator orchestrates the different phases of the release.

The facilitator is the person conversing with the spirit and guiding the discussion. He/she will ask the necessary questions in order to find out what is holding the spirit earthbound. The facilitator guides the conversation and offers healing opportunities to the spirit. The facilitator will be calling to Healing Angels, Transition Angels, and transitioned Loved Ones to assist the spirit with the various phases of the release.

The Medium Role

The medium makes the communication between the spirit and the facilitator possible. The medium is someone who can hear, feel and/or see the spirits.

The medium facilitates the communication in several ways: the medium can relay impressions and images or symbols. They can relay the actual words that the spirit is speaking, or the medium can allow the spirit to use the medium's own voice. We will go more in depth of the different levels of channeling in the following chapters.

Where do you fit in?

As you progress into the advanced stages of working in teams it becomes important to recognize your own inherent natural strengths and limitations. In my own case, I recognize that I cannot see or hear spirits. However, I have learned to sense spirits.

I can often sense the spirit's presence and even the responses to questions or statements. Even with these developed skills, I usually choose to focus on the role of the facilitator and work with a medium. Similarly many mediums choose to focus their skills only as a medium. As each individual develops their individual strengths they have found that their work as a team becomes stronger.

What are your strengths and abilities? Your natural inclinations will point you to the appropriate role. The best teams are those in which each partner has a good knowledge of his/her own skills, abilities and limitations.

As the team proceeds into more advanced work in Soul Rescue and ASR, specialization becomes a key factor in release work. The more each member of the team becomes a master in his/her own chosen role, the more effective the releases become.

On-going Development

It is important to note that inherent psychic skills are required in order to act as a medium. For the purposes of Soul Rescue, full channeling is not necessary. It is enough to relay the imagery, symbolism or the actual words spoken by the spirit.

Mediums desiring to progress into Attached Spirit Release will have ample opportunities for developing the skills required to achieve full channeling.

The role of facilitator requires a basic understanding of human psychology, along with diplomacy and a good sense of humor. Although a Master's degree in counseling is not necessary to help earthbound spirits, some training in counseling or therapy is recommended for complex cases of Soul Rescue and progression into ASR work.

Which one will you be? Explore and have fun!

Chapter 15. The Different Levels of Mediumship within ASR

Levels of mediumship abilities vary greatly from one person to the next. Within Soul Rescue no mediumship skills are required for people working as a facilitator; however, when working with complex cases, a medium team member will be required. In this section we will address the medium and the individual interested in developing his/her existing psychic-medium skills.

Feelings, impressions and images

A first level of mediumship within Soul Rescue is the perception level. The medium will receive impressions and feelings, but may not yet be able to perceive a conversation. The first-level medium is able to feel the presence, or possibly even see the spirit. At this level, communication is symbolic and will require the interpretation from either the medium or the facilitator.

At this level, there may possibly be no clear communication between spirit and facilitator; however, the clues provided in this way by the medium in the form of impressions and symbolism will facilitate the release process. This is a very valid approach to Soul Rescue.

Relaying messages

A more in-depth level of mediumship is through the relaying of messages. At this level, the medium will clearly hear what the spirit is saying and is then able to relay words verbatim to the facilitator.

Being able to relay the spirit's exact words adds tremendous value to the process. The spirit may use a specific word or phrase that has personal or emotional relevance to him/her. The facilitator can then use these words as an entry point to begin addressing the issue that is keeping the spirit trapped in-between worlds.

Channeling

Channeling is the third level of mediumship used in Soul Rescue and in Attached Spirit Release. In this level, the medium fully allows the spirit's personality and words to come through. The spirit will use the medium's own voice apparatus and, to some extent, body gestures.

What are the limits and scope of each?

First Level: Feelings, impressions and images

This type of mediumship is a safe and easy entryway into Soul Rescue and can allow the beginning medium to comfortably explore their skills. This is the perfect way to start for those who are uncertain if they possess mediumship skills.

With this level of mediumship, the work may be limited to mostly wandering earthbound spirits and spirits willing to transition.

Second Level: Relaying information

With this level of mediumship, the medium can work with the entire range of earthbound spirits, from the wandering EB's eager to go to the Light to those more recalcitrant and not necessarily seeking help.

Because the spirit is kept at a distance, by not being connected to the medium, this level of mediumship also allows the beginning medium to explore their own developing skills in a comfortable manner.

The limitation to this method is that the medium must be diligent in relaying the exact words and phrases to the facilitator. Often a change in wording or summary of statements can affect the approach of the release by the facilitator. In this method the facilitator must remember to speak directly to the spirit but listen through the medium.

Third Level: Channeling

This level is the most versatile level of mediumship and allows the medium to work in all aspects of Soul Rescue and advanced Attached Spirit Release.

The primary challenge and limitation of this method is with the adaptability of the medium. In all levels of mediumship there will be a constant learning and personal growth process; however, the channeling-medium will be constantly stretched with each spirit encounter to allow that spirit to fully express their own individual thoughts, emotions and feelings that may be completely foreign to the medium's own natural patterns of thoughts, emotions or feelings. The channeling-medium must be willing to learn to adapt to these changes with each new experience.

Channeling remains the most effective method for Soul Rescue and Attached Spirit Release.

Chapter 16. The Facilitator Role Within ASR

The facilitator is the team member that interacts with the spirit through conversation and helps the spirit to transition. While the medium may interact with the spirit to encourage him/her to speak, it is the facilitator who will be guiding the spirit and coordinating the transition with the help of the Angels and other transitioned loved ones.

The facilitator should always remain in control of the conversation. Through compassionate and casual conversation, the facilitator gathers information about the spirit and the spirit's personality. The facilitator will learn to use targeted questions in order to help the spirit to discover the reason for staying earthbound and to help the spirit to move past the issue in order to transition.

What is the role of a Facilitator?

The role of the facilitator is to coordinate the entire Soul Rescue process, from the initial calling out of the spirit through to the transition.

The facilitator actively listens to the spirit and deciphers the clues as to why the spirit is earthbound and, using tact and diplomacy, helps the spirit face and resolve, or move past, the issue(s) that keeps him/her from transitioning. The facilitator often acts as a pseudo-therapist to the earthbound spirit.

One key aspect to the facilitator role is maintaining order and control over the general proceedings of the release. The spirit may lack focus and may not want to talk about the reasons why they are earthbound, or the spirit may want to talk about an entirely different topic not relevant to the transition. At all times, the facilitator is in control of the conversation and sets the tone for the session in a gentle yet firm manner. It is the responsibility of the facilitator to always bring the conversation back to the desired outcome.

Emotional Security

By maintaining constant control over the situation, the facilitator is establishing the emotional security for the spirit in order to come to accept his/her own death and to accept healing. The established control of the facilitator also lends emotional security to the medium to allow the spirit to fully express a wide range of emotions. It is important to note that the emotions displayed by the spirit may be foreign to the medium, and thus the level of emotional security offered by the facilitator, to the medium, becomes important to the process as a whole.

Remaining in constant control is a mutual and reciprocal responsibility. As the facilitator maintains control of the conversation and guides the spirit on the appropriate path, this in turn makes it easier for the medium to maintain emotional and behavioral control over the spirit, thus making it easier for the facilitator to proceed with the release.

Remember the Outcome

The Soul Rescue team (medium and facilitator) must always know the desired outcome before starting any interaction with a spirit. The goal of Soul Rescue (as taught within this series) is to assist the spirit to transition.

As the working skills of the Soul Rescue team matures, it can become a challenge to not assist the spirit to work through countless issues and challenges that he or she may have experienced over the last, or even previous, incarnation. By remembering that the goal is to assist the spirit to transition, we also place our trust in the guides and advisors of the after-life.

Facilitator Off-target vs. On-target

In my initial sessions in working with a channeling medium, I would often become very involved in assisting the spirit with resolving issues and even sometimes past-life patterns. Although this may have assisted the spirit, it also led to very lengthy sessions.

In one early session the spirit of Jean-Pierre came to us. Jean-Pierre was a very happy man but confessed that he had been mostly a very lazy man throughout his life. He had lived his life with a wife that he didn't love and in a job that he didn't enjoy. He told us that he was simply just too lazy to get a divorce or to find another job. His primary activity, outside of work, was sitting on the couch watching sports on TV and drinking beer. Upon further probing, I found that the root cause of Jean-Pierre's laziness had stemmed from being abandoned by his mother as a child. With the help of the Angels, Jean-Pierre was able to find out that his mother had not abandoned him as he had been led to believe. His mother was sick and left her child in the care of friends while she could heal. She shortly thereafter became terminally ill and passed away, unbeknownst to the caretakers of her son. The friends had merely assumed that his mother had abandoned the child.

In this example, Jean-Pierre came to us ready to transition. If we had only called upon Angels and transitioned loved ones, the session would have been completed within 10 – 15 minutes. As a result of the healing interactions, the session lasted approximately 45 minutes – 1 hour! Although some teams may choose to assist with this level of in-depth healing, we now aspire to assist a greater number of spirits and keep focused on the outcome of transition.

By contrast, I once went to a restaurant with a medium friend of mine. She saw that two spirit children were running around the restaurant and causing havoc for their distraught earthbound mother. Their mother, Magdalena, was reprimanding the two boys, Charles Jr. and Ronald (Ronny), and threatening them with punishment from their father when he returned. Since the boys were also disturbing my friend, she telepathically told them, "You should listen to your mother." The boys were so taken aback at being seen and acknowledged that they went to hide behind the skirt of their mother.

Magdalena came over to our table and apologized for the unruliness of her children. She told us how she was waiting for her husband to come along and she couldn't imagine how he could have been delayed. My friend could see that the mother and her two boys were dressed from a period resembling the early 1800's. Yes, her husband had indeed been delayed for quite some time apparently.

Once my friend relayed the information to me, I offered to call her husband, Charles Sr., to come for his family. Charles Sr. and the Angels of Transition came as requested. Magdalena immediately ran into her husband's arms as Charles Jr. and Ronny each wrapped around one of their father's legs. The family was reunited.

This experience all took place while we were waiting for our order to arrive.

Chapter 17. The Medium Role Within ASR

What does the Medium do?

The medium is the team member that allows the spirit to communicate through him or her. S/he is the person who intimately communicates with the spirit while being privy to thoughts, feelings and memories that only s/he can share with the spirit.

By being in both the physical world and the spirit world, the medium acts as a relay station for the facilitator. By relaying information, or by channeling the spirit, the medium allows the spirit to hold a conversation with the facilitator.

The Value of a Medium

The use of a skilled medium is often discounted. To the casual observer, it may appear that a person channeling is not doing anything. When a skilled medium channels a spirit, it may seem to be a very simple and easy process to the outside observer. The actual work of a skilled medium happens highly unnoticed.

One of the key elements to a good medium is to make the process emotionally safe for the spirit in order to allow him/her to speak through the medium. Unconsciously, the spirit will turn to the medium for emotional safety and reassurance during the session.

Many spirits are not aware that they no longer have a physical body. The facilitator will help the spirit to recognize this fact, but it is the medium that will emotionally support the spirit as s/he goes through this sometimes harsh realization. The medium will assist the spirit through the strong emotional reactions.

A facilitator may suggest ideas or concepts to the spirit that may appear daunting or unsettling. The skilled medium, being able to sense the spirit's fear, will simply sooth and reassure the spirit, thereby making the work of the facilitator easier and also making the process emotionally safer for the spirit.

The facilitator may explain a concept or use a phrase in a way that the spirit doesn't understand. The skilled medium can recognize the thinking patterns of the spirits and identify the spirit's mental and emotional limitations. The medium is always alert to the shifts in emotions or thinking of the spirit and when appropriate, will expand on the explanations given by the facilitator, in order to help the spirit relate and connect with what is being said.

The facilitator may be unaware of the inner dialogue taking place between the medium and the spirit. The only noticeable clue during the session will be when the spirit will seem to be in reflection for a few moments, then will simply accept to move on to the next step suggested by the facilitator. It is during these moments when the medium, sharing the consciousness of the spirit, will reassure or explain concepts in a way that match the spirit's own background.

One day while working with a gifted medium, an earthbound spirit named Winnie came to us. She was a young African girl of about 8 years old. During the session, Patrick told little Winnie that he was going to call on Healing Angels to help her heal her physical body. The medium could sense inside Winnie that the little girl had no clue what Angels were and that she didn't understand who or what I wanted to call for help. She saw within Winnie's memories that in her lifetime, a medicine man, referred to as a "Gri-Gri," performed the healing and various rituals for her people. She told Winnie that I wanted to call on beings that performed similar duties as the Gri-Gri. With this new realization Winnie told me about the great medicine man of her tribe. I then simply asked a transitioned Gri-Gri of Winnie's tribe to come forth and assist in the healing.

As soon as she saw the transitioned Gri-Gri come forth, Winnie was very happy and felt safe. She was then able to turn over whatever residues of pain and trauma were left from her last physical incarnation. When the healing was concluded, it was the Gri-Gri holding little Winnie's hand and escorting her into the Light. This is a perfect example of how the skilled medium will bridge the gap between the facilitator's reality and that of the spirit.

Initial probing for information

Once the medium makes first contact with the spirit there is an opportunity for a brief information exchange that allows the medium to do an initial probing in a casual and respectful manner. The goal of this initial probing is to provide the facilitator with preliminary information about the spirit in order to be able to help the spirit to transition in the most effective and efficient manner.

Once the spirit responds to the facilitator calling out, the medium will acknowledge the spirit then telepathically begin the conversation by asking his or her name. If the medium is able to view the spirit, any descriptive information is also relayed to the facilitator. The physical description of the spirit is usually the appearance just before death and prior to any fatal injuries. Spirits that have died in auto accidents or that have sustained other fatal injuries will rarely appear to the medium in a gory or gruesome manner. The spirit will always appear in the form that his/her personality most identifies with. To most spirits this will be their last intact physical form.

In this initial information exchange it is also helpful if the medium can identify the cause of death. However, sometimes, due to trauma or denial, the medium may not initially have access to that information until the spirit comes to accept being physically deceased.

Medium Summary

If the medium is relaying information, he/she can provide additional information as the conversation unfolds, such as agitation, excitement, confusion, etc. If the medium is channeling the spirit, it then becomes his/her responsibility to ensure that the spirit remains under control and behaves in an appropriate manner. This process happens through communicating with the spirit and setting compassionate, yet firm, ground-rules with the spirit for the conversation.

In this Soul Rescue Manual, you are being given the information and exercises that will allow you to seamlessly progress, as facilitators and mediums, into the practice of Attached Spirit Release. The roles, as defined above, ensure a safe and confident progression into more advanced and complex cases.

Rarely will a Soul Rescue team ever call out a spirit that will be beyond the team's ability to assist that spirit. However, the beginning medium (or even trained medium) and facilitator must learn to recognize when a spirit is beyond their own level of capabilities and refer the case to a more experienced channel or team.

Chapter 18. Interacting with the Spirits

Knowing the Outcome

The primary outcome of any release session is always, assisting and coordinating the spirit through to transition.

Although the facilitator and the medium each have the same goal, both team members will use their own individual methods of assisting the spirit to move towards this outcome.

All parties involved should always keep the outcome in mind when conducting a release session. Is the facilitator asking questions that are getting the spirit closer to that outcome? Although some level of casual conversation is required to establish trust and rapport, as soon as the facilitator is confident in the relationship with the spirit, all questions should be geared towards two goals:

1.   Discovering what is keeping the spirit earthbound;

2.   Helping the spirit resolve enough of the issue that has kept him/her earthbound in order to transition.

Knowing the outcome helps the team stay focused.

What's in the Way?

There is always a reason why a spirit will stay earthbound. Each and every earthbound spirit will have a personal reason why they remained behind; the reason that they did not transition. Very often the reason that they remained behind is not the same reason that they continue to stay earthbound. It is the task of the skilled facilitator to graciously and expeditiously discover the matter that keeps the spirit earthbound.

The key to a successful Soul Rescue is not in finding out why the spirit did not transition; but rather to find out what is keeping the spirit from transitioning.

In the following chapters I'll offer a number ideas and phrases that I've found effective in helping to determine what is keeping the spirit from transitioning; however, each team will need to determine and refine the words and phrases that work best for their own style of communication. With time and practice, each team will identify the key questions and phrases that work best for them.

Please do not be concerned about being able to immediately get to the core of what is keeping the spirit earthbound. Most spirits have no expectations other than being happy to be acknowledged and to finally be able to communicate with someone.

I'm stuck, Now What? - Getting input from the Medium

All facilitators will get stuck at some point during the Soul Rescue attempts.

When the facilitator has depleted his/her personal list of "Standard Spirit Questions" and is not making any further progress, simply ask the spirit to move aside so that the facilitator can speak directly to the medium (in the case of channeling). As the medium returns to consciousness, the medium is then able to share insights about the spirit's thoughts and perspective. With this new information and understanding, the facilitator may then be able to use a different approach to resolving the issue and assist the spirit to transition.

Memory Lapses

Very often a spirit may not remember seemingly important details from his/her lifetime. This can be highly disconcerting to the spirit. In these moments it is important for both the facilitator, and the medium, to downplay this reaction. In most instances it is enough just to ask a different, and unrelated, question.

It is also important to remember that many of the spirits will not be aware that they no longer have a physical body. To understand what the spirit may be feeling, for a moment imagine that someone has asked you something as simple as your last name. Imagine that you don't remember your last name. This can be highly disconcerting, or even frightening to most people. Next imagine that this person asked for the name of the city that you live. Again, you cannot remember either of these seemingly mundane, but important, details. Imagine your own reaction, and then you can imagine the experience of how the spirit may react to these same questions and not being able to recall the answers.

In most cases it will seem to a spirit like only yesterday they were living their normal everyday life and now suddenly they find that they are here talking to you.

"Who are you?"

A common question that spirits may ask is, "Who are you?" This is an understandable question, since we all want to know to whom we are speaking with before divulging too much personal information. Each team will need to determine what feels right for them. I will most often use the phrase, "I'm just someone that likes to help people. Is it okay if I try to help you?" This is usually met by a reluctant affirmation that then allows the session to continue.

Another related common question is, "Are you a ...?" This can be anything from a Priest, Shaman, Magician, Healer, God, etc. It is important to know the implications of answering this question because many of the spirits that will be encountered during the Soul Rescue sessions will be from different time periods, cultures and locations. The facilitator will not necessarily have an understanding of what this label means to the spirit. A standard answer that I will often use to this question is, "What does being a Priest (Shaman, Magician, Healer, etc.) mean to you?" In some cultures when a Priest came for a person it meant that they had been chosen to be the next human sacrifice. It may be useful to know what the term "Priest" means to a spirit before trying to compare the role of facilitator to that of a Priest.

In some cases, "I'm just someone that likes to help people," is not enough. The spirit may be looking for assurances that the facilitator can actually help before they are willing to cooperate. In these cases it becomes necessary to be gently direct with the spirit with regards to physical existence. Once the fact has been established that the spirit no longer has a physical body, they are usually more willing to allow the facilitator to be of assistance.

A typical interaction may proceed as follows.

Facilitator: "I'm someone that specializes in helping people that are in circumstances such as yours."

Spirit: "And what circumstances are those? Am I in some kind of trouble?"

Facilitator: "Are you aware that you no longer have a physical body, but that you do continue to exist?"

Emotional Security

A primary concern in the work of Soul Rescue is the Emotional Security of the spirit involved. Although a spirit may simply be in denial of the death experience, it is very often a traumatic moment when the spirit receives the confirmation that they are indeed dead. It is often even further unsettling to the spirit to learn that the ability to leave the earthbound experience has been available to them all along. In some cases a spirit may have been earthbound for decades or even centuries.

It is the task of the skilled facilitator/medium team to help the spirits to experience these feelings and to assist them to move past them with the help of the Angels. This is done by compassionate listening and reassuring the spirit that they can now move on.

In some cases the spirit will state the reason that they couldn't move on, such as a man who could not leave his wife and family alone and unsupported. Rather than tell the spirit that he should just move on and forget about his family, it is often easier to empathize with the spirit and tell him that it is understandable that he would not want to leave his family. Then, in a compassionate manner, the facilitator may offer to send Angels to the man's family to help them with their burdens. After asking Angels to please watch over and help to comfort and support the family, the facilitator can then ask the spirit if he would like to let go of any remaining guilt so that he can move on unencumbered by these feelings and emotions of guilt.

By always keeping the Emotional Security of the spirit in mind, the team will find that the sessions will progress more smoothly and with less effort than when trying to convince a spirit to move into the Light.

Year of Death

In many cases I'll ask the spirit what is the current year. The reason for this is to establish the time period reference of the spirit. It is often helpful to know that a spirit is hearing everything said in the current conversation, but from the mindset of someone from 1776. In this case there should be no references in the conversation to electrical appliances, lighting or anything that would startle the spirit into the sudden realization that s/he has been wandering for centuries.

If the spirit has not been told that they do not have a physical body at this point it will be important to make light of the question. A typical interaction may be as follows.

Facilitator: "By the way Angela, what year is it?"

Spirit: "What do you mean what year is it? It's the same for you isn't it?"

Facilitator: "Oh I was just making notes and these things always slip my memory. I'm sorry I forget these things sometimes. I know it's silly. What year is it again please?"

In this way a spirit is able to respond to the question without becoming alarmed or defensive. I recommend never telling the spirit the current date or year to avoid any possible traumatic experience for the spirit.

Attached Spirit to the Spirit

In more complex cases it is not unusual to find a spirit that has an attached spirit. Whenever a spirit is unable to transition, or feels that there is something holding him/her back from going into the Light, this is usually a sign that there is an attached spirit preventing the process.

Very often the attached spirit has very honorable intent of wanting to help the host spirit in some way. In other cases the attached spirit is with the host spirit as a form of safety or shelter. Use the same assumptions with the attached spirit as with the host spirit; they are simply lost souls that are confused and wandering.

We will often find karmic connections between the attached spirit and the host spirit; although it is not always necessary take the time to find these connections.

Dark Entities

In the beginning levels of Soul Rescue, you will only be working with wandering earthbound spirits that are willing to transition. If you choose to progress into more challenging areas of Soul Rescue, you may encounter Dark Entities. Dark Entities may sometimes manifest in overly angry or aggressive spirits.

In very few cases, some teams may encounter these entities present in Earthbound Spirits that may be preventing their transition. These spirits may perceive a dark spot or "black thing" inside of themselves. These cases will not be the norm but they are real and they do exist.

In some of these cases the facilitator may assure the spirit that the "dark spot", "thing inside", etc. will not prevent his/her transition. The facilitator will then call upon Healing Angels to help the spirit to understand how s/he can still transition.

51

Once the spirit moves into the Light, the Dark Entity will separate from the spirit and fall away; although in some rare cases it may appear to the spirit that the entity is preventing the transition.

If you encounter such a case of Dark Entity(s) and you are unable to assist the spirit with the help of the Healing Angels, we suggest referring this case to more experienced teams until such a time when your own team has learned to work with releasing these entities in advanced Attached Spirit Release.

In the following chapter the Soul Rescue process is outlined in a Step-By-Step approach.

Chapter 19. Steps of the Soul Rescue

Starting the process

The Facilitator and the Medium will first take a few moments to become centered. The facilitator must be in a "centered" state that allows him or her to speak to spirits in a compassionate and authoritative tonality. The Medium must be able to see, hear and/or sense the responses from the spirit.

1. Take a few moments to breathe and become centered

2. Let go of any fears of the process

3. Let go of any disturbing thoughts or concerns not associated with the task at hand

The next step is inviting angels to be present and asking for protection. This is a precautionary step to prevent the wandering spirits from staying with the person or groups involved with the session. The following script may be used.

"I ask for Healing Angels to please come now and I ask for protection for myself and all that are here so that no new attachments are incurred as a result of the work that we are about to do.

"I ask for Healing Angels and Angels of Transition to please be present for all the spirits that will be called here."

The Interaction

I. Calling Out the Spirit

The facilitator will initiate the interaction by Calling Out to a wandering earthbound spirit that would like to transition, but may need help to do so. The medium is then asked to perceive the spirit that has come in response to the calling. The medium may see, hear or sense the spirit in accordance with his/her own skills.

In the event that the medium reveals that more than one spirit has responded to the invitation, the facilitator may simply narrow the request such as, "we'd like to speak to the youngest (oldest, etc.) spirit."

The facilitator must be mindful to be specific in the invitation, but not so specific as to attempt to call an individual spirit by name.

Example of calling out

"I would like to invite an earthbound spirit to come talk with us that is ready to transition and that would like to transition but that needs help in transitioning. I invite you to come now and speak through (Medium's name). You may speak through him/her, but in no way will you harm or disrupt him/her."

II. Preliminary Information

The medium will then welcome the spirit and probe for preliminary information. This can include, but is not limited to, gender, name, physical appearance, clothes, cause of death, state-of-mind, beliefs and any other information that could prove useful to the facilitator.

III. Addressing the Spirit

The control of the conversation is then turned over to the facilitator. It now becomes the task of the facilitator to engage the spirit in conversation and through the steps to facilitate the release. The facilitator must direct all questions to the spirit and allow the medium to answer for the spirit.

Initially, the beginning medium may only be able to perceive Yes or No responses. In these instances the facilitator must only ask questions that the spirit can answer in Yes/No format. The skilled facilitator must always be mindful of the capabilities and limitations of the medium team member.

IV. Building Rapport

A mistake that is often made by new facilitators is asking questions of the spirit in an Interrogation-manner. A spirit should be treated like an unknown guest at a party. The facilitator should make the spirit feel welcome and safe. A semi-formal greeting followed by mutual introductions is often a nice way to begin conversations with spirits.

The following are some sample questions that we have found useful for establishing rapport.

"Good evening. (pause for reply) My name is Patrick, thank you for coming out to talk with us tonight. May I know your name?"

"Hello Jenny, my name is Patrick, thank you for coming out to talk with us tonight. (pause for reply) How may I help you tonight?"

V. Addressing "Physical Existence"

It is often the case that the spirit will not know, or acknowledge, that s/he is dead. After some preliminary information is exchanged, the facilitator will need to find out if the spirit is aware of being dead. The manner of questioning is extremely important to the emotional-safety of the spirit. This topic should always be introduced with great empathy and in the most delicate manner possible.

We recommend that the spirit NEVER be told, "You're dead"; instead, propose the concept to the spirit in a gentle manner such as, "Are you aware that you no longer have a physical body?" This allows the spirit to sometimes recall the death experience in a detached and emotionally safe manner. This also begins a dialogue of why the spirit chose to stay behind, or what is preventing the spirit from transitioning.

VI. Offering Healing

Often spirits are trapped in the memory of their last moments of life. This can manifest as the spirit being unable to breathe, or being locked in some confined space or area.

In one session, I learned that the spirit was drowned in a river. She had been weighed down with rocks and thrown into the river as a "test" to find out if she had been a witch. Although the spirit had passed the test successfully, wherein they found that she was not a witch, she had died in the river and was trapped in the traumatic moment of her death. She could not breathe nor free herself from the bindings.

The facilitator requested Healing Angels to remove her from the river and to bring her to the shore. The Angels then were asked to remove the bindings and to assist her to breathe normally again. She was then able to converse and was assisted to transition to the Light.

Offering healing accomplishes two important objectives. First, by removing the residues of whatever is bothering the spirit, the spirit is then freed from having to re-experience the karma of the residue in any future reincarnated lifetime. Second, by offering the spirit healing from the Angels, that spirit is then exposed to the nature and feeling of the Angels. This in turn makes the invitation to transition much easier in most cases.

VII. Invitation to Transition

Offering healing is not always necessary. Some spirits are simply just confused and are not aware that they do not have a physical body any longer. When the facilitator informs the spirit that they do not have a physical body, the spirit may seem shocked or in a state of confusion for a moment. The facilitator may then use this as an opportunity to ask the spirit, "Would you like to go with loved ones (mommy, grandma, husband, wife) to a better place where you can rest and feel safe?" If the spirit is willing to transition, simply invite transitioned Loved Ones and, with the help of the Angels of Transition, tell the spirit that he can leave with these guides when s/he is ready.

This invitation can also open a dialogue that begins the process of finding out what is keeping the spirit earthbound. Rather than accepting the invitation to transition, the spirit may begin to share an event or situation from his/her life. The facilitator must take careful notice of what the spirit shares directly after the invitation to transition because this will be the key in helping the spirit to discover what keeps him/her earthbound.

VIII. Finding & Healing the Obstacles to Transition

The solution to the Obstacle-to-Transition is always a core-emotion, regardless of the circumstances that the spirit may present. It is the task of the facilitator to find what is the underlying core-emotion that prevents the spirit from transitioning.

In one Soul Rescue session, eight-year-old little Elizabeth came to us and knew that she was dead. She had told us that she had died by the river after she was thrown from her horse. This seemed like a very simple obstacle. We simply offered to call for her mother to come for her. Elizabeth responded that she did not want her mother to come for her because she was afraid of being punished. She went on to tell us that she had taken her horse out by herself and knew that she wasn't supposed to. We immediately realized that the Core-Emotion was Elizabeth's fear of punishment from her mother. We then invited other Transitioned Loved Ones to come for little Elizabeth. She was able to then transition knowing that she would be safe and well taken care of.

Chapter 20. The Relay Method of Soul Rescue

The Relay Method is based on the facilitator speaking directly to the spirit and the medium relaying the words and emotions of the spirit back to the facilitator.

Once the facilitator invites an earthbound spirit to assist, the medium will give preliminary information as described in previous chapters. The conversation between the facilitator and the spirit will then progress with the medium only acting as a "relay" or translator; from mental words, images or thoughts, to the words spoken to the facilitator.

Considerations in Using the Relay Method

The medium must relay the information as accurately as possible, with little or no "interpretation" of what the spirit is saying. If the spirit is saying, "I was sad that she left," do not say, "The spirit misses her." The differences are sometimes very subtle, but the significance and meaning can have deeper implications.

The medium is not to paraphrase or modify what the spirit is saying. If the sentence is grammatically incorrect, simply relay the message to the facilitator in the same format. Some spirits will have had little or no education and their vocabulary will reflect this speech pattern. Some spirits may speak with slang phrases. Again, the medium should relay the message with the intended slang. This will often help to comfort the spirit that his/her message is being presented in the intended manner. Maintaining the integrity of what the spirit is saying will greatly assist the facilitator to understand the spirit and to adapt the level of conversation to the needs the spirit.

When inviting wandering earthbound spirits to talk, it is an excellent practice to have an empty chair pulled out for the spirit to "sit" in. The facilitator will then address all questions facing the empty chair. The facilitator may however, look at the medium when listening to the spirit's responses.

Chapter 21. The Channeling Method of Soul Rescue

The Channeling Method is based on the facilitator speaking directly to the spirit through the medium. As described in the preceding chapters, the medium is fully aware and conscious of the interactions between the spirit and the facilitator, and will even assist in the process when necessary.

In Soul Rescue sessions, the channeling-medium will have the precious opportunity and privilege of witnessing a small peek into what awaits us all upon death. Each visual experience is unique and personal to the individual spirit, but the feeling and overall experience is always astounding with the sense of Love, acceptance and grace from the Other Side. This experience is a unique and precious opportunity available to anyone with mediumship skills willing to participate in the Soul Rescue process.

For the first-time channeling-medium, simply getting started may be a challenge. It is noteworthy that many first-time mediums have stated that, "the first few words are always the hardest." Initially, the medium will learn only to become relaxed enough to allow the spirit to speak, while still remaining a conscious influence in the process.

Imagination also plays a key aspect for the first-time medium. In the beginning it may seem as though the imagination of the medium is creating the entire "Spirit Experience." However, in time and with many confirmations later, the medium will begin to trust that there is a very thin distinction between the veil of imagination and actual experience. I suggest that the first-time medium allow the experience to unfold, even while this may still seem like a story produced from within his/her own mind.

Seeing It Through

Once the spirit has agreed to leave with Transitioned Loved Ones and/or Angels of Transition, the medium will continue to keep contact with the spirit until the spirit has entered fully into the Light. As the spirit is escorted into the Light, the medium may perceive a "tunnel of Light", or a "staircase going up to the Light", or any number of other symbolic transition visions. During this last step, and at some point, the medium will find that the consciousness will be "disengaged" from that of the spirit. The process may feel to the medium as though someone from the other side is saying, "This is as far as you're allowed to go." It is at this point when the medium can be fully assured that the spirit is in full care of the Other Side. The medium will then return to full consciousness and may share with the facilitator what has transpired.

Channeling the Spirit vs. Becoming the Spirit

A common mistake among new channeling mediums is to identify too closely with the spirit for whom they are channeling. When channeling a spirit it is important to keep a distinct sense of self, apart from the identity of the spirit. This will help when it becomes necessary to assist the facilitator in relaying the thought patterns and emotions of the spirit. When the medium associates too closely with the spirit this, in turn, becomes a burden because the medium begins to have the same emotional issues during the session as the spirit. The medium will then be unable to assist the facilitator in the most effective manner.

Although the medium may feel great empathy and compassion for the spirit, by keeping in an "observer" position, the medium can then be of greatest to service in assisting the spirit to transition.

Other Considerations in Using the Channeling Method

In her book, *"Remote Depossesion,"* Dr. Irene Hickman outlines how, under hypnosis, anyone who is a good hypnotic subject can be used as a channel for earthbound spirits and entities. This is an excellent book that I recommend to anyone wanting to learn more about Soul Rescue and Attached Spirit Release; although I do not entirely agree with the late Dr. Hickman that hypnotic subjects should be used as channels in this work.

When a person with latent mediumship talents chooses to participate in Soul Rescue, this can be a tremendous service to the world in helping countless Lost Souls in transitioning to the Light. By continuing on to Attached Spirit Release, the blossoming medium can even further assist countless living people that are hosts to various earthbound spirits or other entities. We fully encourage anyone with even perception mediumship skills to become active in this work.

In the next chapter we will explore the active role that a medium can play in the Soul Rescue process.

Chapter 22. Becoming an Effective Channeling Medium

What exactly is an Effective Channeling Medium? There is a simple rule: the more effective the channel, the less "filtering" the medium will do.

When channeling a spirit, the spirit will use some of the medium's own mental constructs and speech patterns. This will also sometimes include the medium's own personal beliefs and self-imposed limitations, which act as "filters" for the spirit's communication. This is a very normal process and should not be viewed as cause for invalidating the process. However, the channeling medium becomes most effective when the spirit is using as little as possible of the medium's own personal makeup.

To become an Effective Channeling Medium, the medium should continually strive for increasingly becoming a clear channel in Soul Rescue.

Self-Development as a Medium

The skill of channeling, like any other, is in constant evolution and progress. The very act of engaging in a channeling session redefines who the medium is, pushing back the medium's perceived limits and beliefs in order to accommodate the spirits that are channeled.

As each spirit is channeled by the medium, each session must be viewed as a new and unique experience. This can be compared to an initial meeting of a new person. Although it may be a familiar experience to meet new people, each experience is unique. How each spirit will present him/herself is the mystery that the medium must be prepared to receive.

The joy of mediumship is the constant redefining of the Self by allowing each unique spirit's personality to be channeled and assisted to transition. It is the privilege and the honor of the channeling medium to have a brief, yet intimate, relationship with the spirit and to experience a glimpse into the joy of the after-life.

Preferences & Prejudices

A key to becoming an effective channel is to hold no prejudice over any spirit who asks for help. The medium (or facilitator) that desires to be of the highest service cannot allow preferences or prejudices to interfere with the work of Soul Rescue. Spirits of various morals, deeds, accomplishments, races, gender, creed, religion, sexual preference, and etc. all need help.

In various sessions with mediums, we have assisted a man that was hanged for murder, and in other session a man that was murdered. We have witnessed angels heal and escort the spirit of a mobster, and we have witnessed the angels do the same for a man shot and killed during a robbery. We watched the angels heal and care for the spirit of the sailor who had venereal disease, even though he knowingly spread it to many women. They also healed the spirit of a woman who had died of an accidental drug overdose given to her from her, "boyfriend for the night." In each of these experiences the angels were equally loving and non-judgmental, as we hope that we can all be during each Soul Rescue session.

Most spirits that come for help will not be "happy". The majority of earthbound spirits that we have encountered have been unhappy, depressed, anxious, angry, frustrated, or simply just confused. The medium cannot judge of the "quality" of the spirit. Happy spirits are not better than angry or depressed spirits, they each simply have different issues. The role of the medium is to facilitate communication between the spirit and the facilitator, and to assist the spirit to transition back to the Light.

The Active Role of the Medium

The medium will have opportunities to provide the spirit with additional explanations. The facilitator may phrase statements in a way that the spirit doesn't understand, or has no reference. The skilled medium recognizes the thinking patterns of the spirit and identifies the spirit's mental and emotional limitations.

The medium is always paying attention to the shifts in emotions or thinking of the spirit and when appropriate, will expand on the explanations given by the facilitator in order to help the spirit relate and connect with what is being said.

Precious information can also be given to the facilitator about the spirit's beliefs or state of mind or limitations.

In one particular session, a spirit that came that appeared to be a Viking warrior. The medium could see that his mind was organized very simply, not that the spirit was stupid, but that his life had been very simple. He was a man and a warrior, end of story. His roles and duties were clearly defined and he went through life with little existential questioning; all of his energy had been focused on survival and providing for his family. This information had been relayed to me prior to starting the session.

Very early into the session the medium could perceive that the Viking warrior was becoming agitated that I was speaking to him, in the warrior's opinion, as a stupid man. His ego was being hurt simply because I was speaking to him very slowing. The medium interrupted the session before the situation escalated. She could perceive the spirit becoming very hurt and agitated, unbeknownst to me.

She then clarified that "simple" meant that his life and mind were not complex but that the Viking was not stupid. I was informed to keep the content of his speech simple, but not speak to the warrior like a mentally challenged person. I apologized to the spirit then resumed the session with normal speech patterns and in a context that the warrior could relate to. The rest of the session unfolded easily and we were able to help the Viking to transition with his pride intact.

Creating a Light-Space

The channeling-medium's true role is to "contain" the spirit within his/her energy field. The experienced Soul Rescue medium will not only allow the spirit to speak through him/her, but also creates a space within him/herself to hold the spirit. From this space the spirit is then allowed to use the voice faculties, and limited gestures, of the medium.

While the spirit is in this space the medium is in control of the spirit. The spirit is not allowed to invade the body or mind of the medium; the spirit is limited to that holding space. This holding space provides for a safe interaction between the spirit and medium, it is a common shared space. This is where they share consciousness without merging consciousness. It is this subtle, but important distinction that prevents the spirit from becoming attached to the medium.

The space is filled with light and could be compared to a light bubble or a light-net. Metaphorically speaking, the size of the "light-space" a medium can master will determine the personality type of the spirit that can be channeled by the medium.

For example, a beginning medium with limited experience may only have a small light-space. This space may easily accommodate earthbound spirits willing to transition, but may become insufficient when dealing with stubborn, or angry spirits attached to a location or a person.

The level of a spirit's emotions will usually determine the "size" of a spirit and the size of the light-space required. As an example, a spirit that is angry at the cause of his death may require a light-space of "Size 8". If the medium's current light-space ability is "Size 8", the session will probably leave the medium exhausted and drained of energy. In this example the medium would be using the full extent of the light-space.

By contrast, however, the larger the inner light-space, the less energy is required by the medium to channel the spirit. In a different example, a spirit may simply have died unexpectedly and is confused about why no one can see or hear her. In this example the spirit may only require a light-space of "Size 2". If the medium's current light-space ability were a "Size 8", the session would leave the medium with very little change in energy from the start of the session.

As the student-medium continues to practice channeling earthbound spirits with various personalities, this inner light-space will continue to expand and allow the medium to progress into more advanced spheres of Attached Spirit Release.

Deep-Trance Mediumship vs. Conscious-Trance Mediumship

In the work of Soul Rescue, and related Attached Spirit Release, we do not recommend Deep-Trance Mediumship, but rather the lighter Conscious-Trance Mediumship.

Deep-Trance Mediumship is the act of the medium allowing his/her consciousness to "step aside" while the spirit is then allowed to use the voice faculties and gestures of the medium. It is the belief of many professional mediums that Deep Trance Mediumship provides the most accurate and unbiased information to be delivered since the conscious mind of the medium does not interfere in the process.

Conscious-Trance, or Light-Trance Mediumship is the act of the medium allowing the spirit to use the voice faculties and limited gesturing while the medium remains conscious of the process. The value of Conscious-Trance Mediumship in working with earthbound spirits is that it allows the medium to channel the spirits under controlled supervision. This also provides the medium the ability to interact with the spirit to provide clarification, or to sometimes just provide reassurance.

A Conscious-Trance Medium can also interact with the facilitator. It is not unusual for a facilitator to become confused or "stuck" while attempting to assist a spirit to transition. By asking the Conscious-Trance Medium to return, the facilitator can then ask pertinent questions and the medium can offer insights and observations of the spirit. It is for these reasons that I don't suggest Deep-Trance Mediumship during Soul Rescue.

Ground Rules for Communication

When working in Soul Rescue, it is important to remember that the earthbound spirits to be helped continue to retain their previous life-personality. These spirits are not necessarily more enlightened than the average person. Nor will the spirit be more loving than the average person simply because s/he is dead. By contrast, many (if not most) of the earthbound spirits that the Soul Rescue teams will encounter will be confused, upset, frustrated or angry. It is the goal of the team to assist these spirits to transition, despite the prevailing initial emotions that the spirit may display.

There is a delicate balance between allowing the spirit to express him/herself and maintaining control over how it is done. The spirit should be allowed to freely express him/herself, but without ever being allowed to lash out at the facilitator in any inappropriate manner. It is perfectly normal for some spirits to be angry or bitter, or any other strong negative emotion. It is NOT ever permissible for the spirit to be outwardly hostile or disrespectful to the facilitator, or to the medium in an internal dialogue.

When channeling the spirit, it becomes the medium's responsibility to ensure that the spirit behaves in an appropriate manner. Conversely, it is the responsibility of the facilitator to always remain respectful to every spirit during the Soul Rescue process. The medium must be able to rely on the facilitator to never provoke a spirit or cause the spirit to feel defensive and thus desire to, or impulsively, lash out.

The medium only asserts him/herself if the spirit begins to act disrespectful or hostile in any manner. This assertion happens by communicating to the spirit, in a firm and compassionate manner, that all communications must be kept civil and respectful or the communication ends.

The spirit should also never be allowed to ever control or abuse the medium's physical body. It is never appropriate for the spirit to take control of the medium's physical body. During a Soul Rescue or ASR session, a medium should never experience jerking movements, nervous ticks, convulsions or any other sign of uncontrolled behavior during channeling. If any of these conditions are present, the medium should immediately break communication with the spirit in order to firmly assert proper communications etiquette. In the event that the medium is unaware of these behaviors, it then becomes the responsibility of the facilitator to gently assist the medium to disengage the spirit and return to full consciousness.

There is always a reason why a spirit may be emotionally out-of-control. During the course of the release session it will be the task of the facilitator to discover these reasons and, with the help of the Angels and the medium, to assist the spirit to release these issues. Once these issues have been released, the spirit will then typically become settled and even-tempered.

The medium will learn to recognize when a spirit may be too much (anger, fear, etc.) for the medium's current level of channeling skills. If a medium should ever encounter a spirit that cannot be controlled (i.e. uncontrolled body movements, abusive language, etc.), the medium should break contact from the spirit and either take a short recess, or refer the case to a more experienced channel.

Above all, enjoying what you do is key. Spirits can perceive when a medium enjoys the process and this adds to their emotional security during the release. It is important for the medium to always remember that s/he is there to assist the Lost Soul to transition to a better place.

Appendix A. Classroom Exercises & Scripts

Section 5. & 8. Calling Out Wandering Earthbound Spirits (EB's)

This exercise will be inviting earthbound spirits to come and so that they can be assisted to transition. As your skills progress you will learn the importance of each part of the script so that intent can be applied as you perform the steps in subsequent sessions.

The first part of this exercise is a very key aspect of the process. You must be in a "centered" state that will allow you to speak to spirits in a compassionate and authoritative tonality.

1.   Take a few moments to breathe and become centered

2.   Let go of any fears of the process

3.   Let go of any disturbing thoughts or concerns not associated with the task at hand

The next step is inviting angels to be present and asking for protection. This is a precautionary step to prevent the wandering spirits from staying with the person or groups involved with the session.

Proceed with reading from the script.

Section 5. & 8.   Calling Out Wandering Earthbound Spirits (EB's)

Sample prayer/request - Calling Out to Release Wandering Earthbound Spirits

I.   Prepare Yourself Mentally and Emotionally

II.   The Script

"I ask for Healing Angels and Guardian Angels to please come now and I ask for protection for myself and all that are here so that no new attachments are incurred as a result of the work that we are about to do.

"I ask for Healing Angels and Angels of Transition to please come now and be present for all the spirits that will be called here tonight.

"I now invite any spirits that would like help in transitioning and are ready to transition to please come now.

"I ask that all the Earthbound Spirits here be told, in a way that they can understand, that their physical bodies are no longer in existence but that they continue to exist.

"I ask that they be told, in a way that they can understand, that they are worthy and deserving of going to the Light and that there is no judgment waiting for them except that which they put on themselves.

"I ask that they be helped now to release any judgment on themselves and allow the angels to take away the hurt, guilt and judgments.

"I further ask the angels to please heal each one of any past residues from their death so that they need not experience any symptoms in any future life. I ask that the angels please heal any their aches and sorrows and I invite all you spirits to let go of your hurts, depression or any other pains to the angels.

I now invite all the spirits here to forgive those that they feel they need to forgive from any hurt in the past. Allow the angels to help you with whoever needs to be forgiven so that you can easily move on.

"I now call upon angels of transition and transitioned loved ones to lovingly come for all the spirits here and escort them to the Light.

"Thank you.

"Angels, I ask now that you please remove any residues left by any of the spirits from this space and from myself and all those present. Thank you. Amen"

Section 10. Releasing EB's From A Home or Property

This exercise will be reaching out to earthbound spirits trapped in a home or property to transition. As the class progresses you will learn the importance of each part of the script so that proper intent can be applied as the facilitator performs the steps in subsequent sessions.

The Exercise

This exercise will be done in teams of "Client" and "Facilitator".

The Client will focus on his/her home (or a home that s/he is intimately familiar with).

The Facilitator will release the EB's from the Client's home (or a home that s/he is intimately familiar with).

Client; focus on the home and give a brief description to the facilitator.

Facilitator; follows the intent of the client's focus to the home.

Optionally the facilitator can pretend that s/he can see the client's home. Ask the client for more details if necessary. The intent of the facilitator is to call Angels to that home and to speak to the spirits living in, trapped, or attached in that home.

The first part of this exercise is a very key aspect of the process. In this exercise, both the Client and the Facilitator must take time before starting to become centered. The Client must visualize, or sense, his/her home or location. The facilitator must be in a "centered" state that allows him or her to speak to spirits in a compassionate and authoritative tonality.

1.   Take a few moments to breathe and become centered

2.   Let go of any fears of the process

3.   Let go of any disturbing thoughts or concerns not associated with the task at hand

68

The next step is inviting angels to be present and asking for protection. This is a precautionary step to prevent the wandering spirits from staying with the person or groups involved with the session.

Proceed with reading from the script.

Section 10. Releasing EB's From A Home or Property

Sample prayer/request - Calling Out to Release Earthbound Spirits from a home or property

I.   Prepare Yourself Mentally and Emotionally

II.   The Script

"I ask for Healing Angels and Guardian Angels to please come now and I ask for protection for myself and all that are here so that no new attachments are incurred as a result of the work that we are about to do.

"I ask for Healing Angels and Angels of Transition to please come now to the home of (client's name) and be present for all the spirits here.

"I now invite all the spirits here in the home of (client's name) to make their presence known to the angels.

"I ask that all the Earthbound Spirits here be told, in a way that they can understand, that their physical bodies are no longer in existence but that they continue to exist.

"I ask that they be told, in a way that they can understand, that they are worthy and deserving of going to the Light and that there is no judgment waiting for them except that which they put on themselves.

"I ask that they be helped now to release any judgment on themselves and allow the angels to take away the hurt, guilt and judgments.

"I further ask the angels to please heal each one of any past residues from their death so that they need not experience any symptoms in any future life. I ask that the angels please heal any their aches and sorrows and I invite all you spirits to let go of your hurts, depression or any other pains to the angels.

"I also now invite all the spirits here to forgive those that they feel they need to forgive from any hurt in the past. Allow the angels to help you with whoever needs to be forgiven so that you can easily move on.

"I now call upon angels of transition and transitioned loved ones to lovingly come for all the spirits here and escort them to the Light.

"Thank you.

"Angels, I ask now that you please remove any residues left by any of the spirits from this space and from myself and all those present. Thank you. Amen"

Section 12. Calling Out Attached EB's

This exercise will be reaching out to earthbound spirits attached to a living person. As the class progresses you will learn the importance of each part of the script so that intent can be applied as you perform the steps in subsequent sessions.

The Exercise

This exercise will be done in teams of "Client" and "Facilitator".

The Facilitator will release any earthbound spirits willing to transition with the help of angels and transitioned loved ones.

Client: At the appropriate point of the script, the client will speak directly to the spirits attached to him or her. S/he will give thanks to the spirits that had the intent of trying to help. S/he will then make the statement that s/he is now willing to take responsibility for his/her own life and give his/her permission and blessings for the attached spirits to leave with the angels.

Facilitator: With this exercise it is the job of the Facilitator to make the spirits feel SAFE. The exercise is not attempting to "evict" the spirits from their home within the client. The first step is to offer the spirits help and healing from the angels. Remember, very often spirits have the intent of trying to help. Honor and respect that intent.

The first part of this exercise is a very key aspect of the process. The facilitator must be in a "centered" state that allows him or her to speak to spirits in a compassionate and authoritative tonality.

1. Take a few moments to breathe and become centered

2. Let go of any fears of the process

3. Let go of any disturbing thoughts or concerns not associated with the task at hand

The next step is inviting angels to be present and asking for protection. This is a precautionary step to prevent the wandering spirits from staying with the person or groups involved with the session.

Proceed with reading from the script.

Section 12. Calling Out Attached EB's

Prepare Yourself Mentally and Emotionally

Facilitator Script

"I ask for Healing Angels to please come now and I ask for protection for myself and all that are here so that no new attachments are incurred as a result of the work that we are about to do.

"I ask for Healing Angels and Angels of Transition to please be present for all the spirits that will be called out from (client's name).

"I'm now speaking to all you spirits inside of (client's name) that resonate with the feeling of _____. I know that many of you are with (client's name) to help him/her in some way or in some cases to feel safe or protected. I'm inviting you now to receive healing from the angels that are here before you."

Client Permission to Release

"I'd like to acknowledge all the spirits within me. I know that many of you have come in order to try to help me in your own way. I want to thank you now for your intent of trying to help me.

I want you to know that I am now willing to take responsibility for my own life and I now give you my permission and my blessings to leave with the loving care of the angels."

Facilitator Script (cont.)

"I ask that all the Earthbound Spirits here, and especially the spirits that resonate with the feeling of _____, within (client's name) be told, in a way that they can understand, that their physical bodies are no longer in existence but that they continue to exist.

"I ask the angels to please heal each one of any past residues from their death so that they need not experience any symptoms in any future life. I ask that the angels please heal all of their aches and sorrows and I invite all you spirits to let go of your hurts, depression or any other pains to the angels.

"I ask that they be told, in a way that they can understand, that they are worthy and deserving of going to the Light and that there is no judgment waiting for them except that which they put on themselves.

"I ask that they be helped now to release any judgment on themselves and allow the angels to take away the hurt, guilt and judgments.

"I also now invite all the spirits within (client's name) to forgive those that they feel they need to forgive from any hurt in the past. Allow the angels to help you with whoever needs to be forgiven so that you can easily move on.

"I now call upon angels of transition and transitioned loved ones to lovingly come for all those here and escort them to the Light.

"And as the spirits leave from (client's name), I further ask the angels to please remove the residues from all that has left and fill those spaces with God's Love and God's Light.

"Angels, I ask now that you please remove any residues left by any of these spirits from (client's name), this space and from myself and all those present.

"Angels I ask that (client's name) suffer no ill effects in either general well being or in physical health. I also ask that if any soul fragments are available or any pieces that they be cleaned and reintegrated at their own pace or entrusted to the angels for integration at a later time when (client's name) is ready them. Thank you, Amen."

Bibliography

Baldwin, William, Ph.D., Healing Lost Souls: Releasing Unwanted Spirits from Your Energy Body. Hampton Roads Publishing Company 2003

Baldwin, William, Ph.D., Spirit Releasement Therapy: A Technique Manual. Headline Books; 2nd edition 1995

Browne, Sylvia, Sylvia Browne's Book of Angels. Hay House 2004.

Ireland-Frey, Louise, Freeing the Captives: The Emerging Therapy of Treating Spirit Attachment. Hampton Roads Publishing Company 1999

Moody, Dr. Raymond, Life After Life: The Investigation of a Phenomenon -Survival of Bodily Death. Harper San Francisco; 2nd edition 2001

Hickman, Irene, D.O., Remote Depossesion. Hickman Systems; 2nd edition 1997

Virtue, Doreen, Healing With The Angels. Hay House 1999.

www.SoulRescueSite.com

My own website supporting the work of Soul Rescue and assisting Earthbound Spirits transition, or Cross-Over to the Light.

Printed in Great Britain
by Amazon.co.uk, Ltd.,
Marston Gate.